BE AN

AEROSPACE ENGINEER

BY ZELDA SALT

Gareth Stevens
PUBLISHING

Please visit our website, www.garethstevens.com. For a free color catalog of all our high-quality books, call toll free 1-800-542-2595 or fax 1-877-542-2596.

Library of Congress Cataloging-in-Publication Data

Names: Salt, Zelda, author.
Title: Be an aerospace engineer / Zelda Salt.
Description: New York : Gareth Stevens Publishing, [2019] | Series: Be a
    scientist | Includes index.
Identifiers: LCCN 2018023548| ISBN 9781538229996 (library bound) | ISBN
    9781538231210 (pbk.) | ISBN 9781538231272 (6 pack)
Subjects: LCSH: Aerospace engineering–Vocational guidance–Juvenile
    literature.
Classification: LCC TL850 .S25 2019 | DDC 629.4023–dc23
LC record available at https://lccn.loc.gov/2018023548

First Edition

Published in 2019 by
Gareth Stevens Publishing
111 East 14th Street, Suite 349
New York, NY 10003

Copyright © 2019 Gareth Stevens Publishing

Designer: Katelyn E. Reynolds
Editor: Monika Davies

Photo credits: Cover, p. 1 (main) mihailomilovanovic/E+/Getty Images; cover, p. 1 (screen illustration) shaineast/Shutterstock.com; cover, pp. 1–32 (background image) Bubushonok/Shutterstock.com; p. 5 Stocktrek Images/Getty Images; pp. 7, 21, 29 courtesy of NASA; p. 9 Monty Rakusen/Cultura/Getty Images; p. 11 serato/Shutterstock.com; pp. 13, 23 Erik Simonsen/Photographer's Choice/Getty Images; p. 15 courtesy of NASA Langley Research Center; p. 17 Hero Images/Getty Images; p. 19 NASA/Bryan Allen/Corbis Documentary/Getty Images; p. 25 Caiaimage/Martin Barraud/Getty Images; p. 27 Kathleen Finlay/Image Source/Getty Images.

Printed in the United States of America

CPSIA compliance information: Batch #CW19GS: For further information contact Gareth Stevens, New York, New York at 1-800-542-2595.

CONTENTS

WORDS IN THE GLOSSARY APPEAR IN **BOLD** TYPE
THE FIRST TIME THEY ARE USED IN THE TEXT.

To Infinity AND BEYOND!

People in ancient societies told stories about the night sky. They gave names to constellations, or groups of stars, as a way to give some kind of order to the massive night sky. Who among us hasn't looked up at the stars and wondered what it would be like to visit them?

Aerospace **engineers** do more than wonder. They are the brains behind the **technology** that brought us to the moon and **unmanned** aircraft even further. Sometimes they work on avionics, or the computer systems that spacecraft use. They may also figure out what materials should be used to build spacecraft. If all of this sounds complicated, well...it *is* rocket science!

THE APOLLO PROGRAM

The Apollo program was America's attempt to be the first country to put a person on the moon. There were 17 missions in all. Apollo 11 was the first to succeed. On the Apollo 11 mission, Neil Armstrong was the first person to walk on the moon. He said the famous words, "One small step for a man, one giant leap for mankind." Many aerospace engineers were needed to make that possible!

ON JULY 16, 1969, APOLLO 11 LAUNCHED INTO SPACE. ON JULY 20, THE MISSION LANDED ON THE MOON.

5

LOTS TO LEARN

Engineering objects that will stay on Earth is hard enough. If you are working in aerospace engineering, there is even more to consider!

An aerospace engineer needs a good understanding of chemistry, **physics**, and even human biology! To build a spacecraft, an aerospace engineer should understand the people who will be flying it. For example, what kind of environment can this person live in? What materials should you use to protect them? Aerospace engineers spend a lot of time thinking about these important questions.

Additionally, aerospace engineers have to think about what materials will survive in space. They might study how to push a rocket forward in an environment with no **gravity**.

SPACE EXPLORER AND AEROSPACE ENGINEER

Neil Armstrong was the first man to set foot on the moon, but did you know that before his time on the moon, Armstrong was an aerospace engineer? He was proud of his engineering past, saying, "I am, and ever will be, a white-socks, pocket-protector, nerdy engineer."

There are many specializations you can study in the field of aerospace engineering. Since there is such a wide range, aerospace engineers-in-training will want to study many different kinds of subjects.

For example, you can focus on engineering research and development, or the process of creating something over time and making sure it works. This could include learning how to improve a spacecraft's navigation system, or technology that allows a spacecraft to plot and follow a path from one place to another. You could also go into testing and maintenance, or the practice of caring for something by making repairs and changes when needed.

TESTING, TESTING, 123

Lots of tests and practices must be done before a spaceship can launch. Each piece of a rocket goes through many trials before being put into the final design. Testing is an important part of the engineering process to make sure everyone stays safe and the mission is a success.

ENGINEERS THAT WORK IN TESTING MAY ALSO LOOK AT AIR CRASHES, ROCKET FAILURES, OR OTHER ONBOARD **ACCIDENTS**.

ENGINEERS GET DEGREES

If you're interested in aerospace engineering, you'll want to take chemistry, physics, and math classes in high school. When you get to college, you can major in engineering. At some colleges, you can even major in aerospace engineering.

Aerospace engineering classes will cover many details about flight. You'll learn how to plan a path to travel in space and how to make a spacecraft move. You will also have classes on aerodynamics, or how an aircraft or spacecraft will interact with the air and wind when it flies. You'll also learn more about how flight is affected by thermodynamics, or the ways different forms of energy interact.

ADVANCED DEGREES

If you'd like to make yourself an even stronger candidate for an aerospace engineering job, you may want to get an advanced degree, such a master's degree or a PhD. A master's degree usually takes around 2 to 3 years to complete, but a PhD can take up to 8 years to finish.

CHECK "A" FOR "AEROSPACE"

Are you wondering if aerospace engineering is for you? Take our quiz!
If you answered more than half of the questions with a "yes,"
then aerospace engineering might be for you.

1. Are you interested in outer space?

2. Do you like to take things apart and put them back together?

3. Do you wonder about life on other planets?

4. Are you interested in understanding what makes vehicles move, and why?

5. Are you willing to spend long hours testing new ideas?

6. Do you enjoy working as part of a team?

7. Are you always trying to find better ways to do things?

8. Do you seek adventure?

9. Are you patient, or able to wait a long time, when solving problems?

ASTRO VS. AERO

There are two types of aerospace engineers. Aeronautical engineers and astronautical engineers are both closely related in the field of aerospace.

"Astro" comes from the Greek word meaning "star." "Nautical" means having to do with ships. It makes sense, then, that astronautical engineers build spacecraft, or technology that will fly among the stars.

Astronautical engineers research, design, test, and maintain spacecrafts and technology that will be leaving Earth's atmosphere, or the mixture of gases that surround our planet. They also study the environment that space-bound technology will have to survive in. For example, astronautical engineers may track space weather patterns.

MATH AND TECHNOLOGY

A strong background in math is necessary for aerospace engineering. Astronautical engineers use math to figure out how a spacecraft will leave Earth's atmosphere. They do this by answering questions about distance, speed, and flight paths—all of which need math skills! In many ways, math is the "language" of engineering.

13

"Aero" comes from the Greek word meaning air. Aeronautical engineers design, test, maintain, and improve aircraft, such as planes, that stay inside Earth's atmosphere. But aircraft are different from spacecraft for many reasons. For engineers, the key difference is that there is no air in space. Spacecraft can't fly the same way that aircraft do. An aeronautical engineer can figure out how to use wind to lift an aircraft off the ground, but an astronautical engineer will have to find a way for spacecraft to create their own lift, using engines.

Aeronautical and astronautical engineers face different challenges, or tests of their abilities. However, they have similar jobs and both use the ideas of physics to create their designs.

MARY JACKSON, PIONEER

In 1958, Mary Jackson became NASA's first black, female aerospace engineer. It took a lot of hard work for Jackson to get the job. She had to get special permission to attend night classes in engineering. During her time at NASA, Jackson wrote many research reports that looked at how spacecraft interacted with the air.

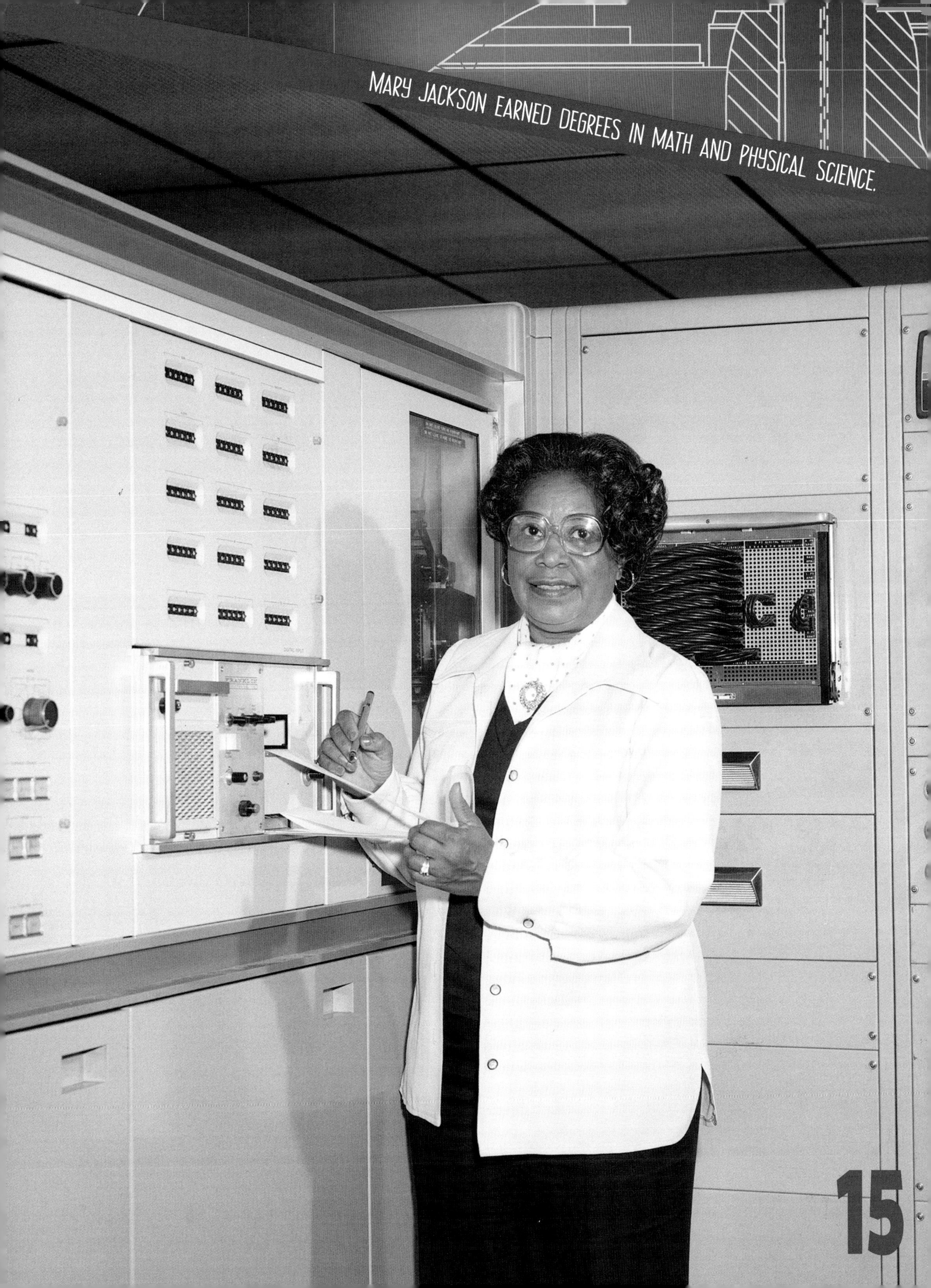

MARY JACKSON EARNED DEGREES IN MATH AND PHYSICAL SCIENCE.

ALL IN A DAY'S WORK

What does a day in the life look like for an aerospace engineer? It depends on what the engineer's specialty is. But for many, the job includes looking at data and solving equations. Aerospace engineers may write technical papers, or research papers explaining what they've learned. They also work with other researchers to build on what they know.

MANAGING THE MECHANICS

Are you interested in aerospace engineering, but not in the **mechanical** side of things? You still have options! Engineers with an advanced degree can become college professors. Or engineers who like more hands-on work can go into project management, with a focus on aerospace engineering. Project managers help organize research, manage people, and work with clients.

Other times, aerospace engineers help test new technology. They will write out engineering processes, or the series of steps or actions taken to make something. Aerospace engineers may travel to launch sites or airports to install new computer programs or software.

MANY AEROSPACE ENGINEERS USE MATH IN THEIR EVERYDAY WORK TO FIGURE OUT THINGS SUCH AS SPEED AND TRAJECTORY, OR THE ROUTE THAT SOMETHING MOVES ALONG THROUGH AIR AND SPACE.

17

WHO'S THE BOSS?

When people think of who hires aerospace engineers, many first think of NASA (the National Aeronautics and Space Administration). NASA is part of the US government and deals with US space technology, as well as works with other space agencies from other countries.

But the aerospace field is growing quickly. Job opportunities outside of NASA are becoming more widely available. Airlines looking to improve or update their aircraft hire aerospace engineers. Some private companies are thinking of how to help more people travel to space. These companies all have different goals. Some focus on how to build high-tech telescopes, while others are looking at how to put people on Mars!

THE SPACE LAUNCH SYSTEM ROCKET

In 2018, NASA tested the world's most powerful rocket. This rocket is designed to carry humans past the moon to planets such as Mars, or even deep space. To do this, NASA's aerospace engineers have been designing a rocket that can achieve a very strong thrust, or force that pushes a rocket forward.

BREAKING DOWN A SPACE SHUTTLE

BELOW IS A DIAGRAM OF A SPACE SHUTTLE THAT ONCE TOOK ASTRONAUTS INTO SPACE. THIS SPACE SHUTTLE HAS THOUSANDS OF PARTS. AEROSPACE ENGINEERS DESIGNED AND TESTED EVERY PART SO THE SPACE SHUTTLE COULD SAFELY HEAD INTO SPACE.

SPEED BRAKE

FORWARD CONTROL THRUST

CARGO BAY

FLIGHT DECK

MAIN ENGINES

DELTA WING

Try and Fail
AND TRY AGAIN

An important **characteristic** that all aerospace engineers share is their refusal to give up. There have been many failures in the history of space flight, but aerospace engineers often learn more from their failures than their successes!

Sometime around 400 BC, one of the first rocket-like machines was launched. However, the first **satellite** to travel in a circle around Earth didn't launch until 1957. This means there have been thousands of years of trial and error!

Aerospace engineers are never happy with technology that's simply "good enough." The best engineers are always trying to find new and better ways to get aircraft and spacecraft flying.

WINGS AND STEAM

Aulus Gellius, a Roman living around 400 BC, wrote about the first rocket-like machine. This machine was a little wooden bird! A Greek named Archytas wanted to do something interesting for his neighbors to watch. So, he hung a wooden bird up on wires and made it "fly" using steam to push the bird forward.

ARCHYTAS'S LITTLE WOODEN BIRD USED IDEAS
AEROSPACE ENGINEERS APPLIED TO THE FIRST ROCKET FLIGHTS!

21

SHIPS AND SATELLITES

Some aerospace engineers focus on vehicles, such as rockets and planes, that can carry people or cargo on flights. Others focus less on vehicles and more on tools and technology. This technology includes satellites that help us in our daily lives. These satellites help us get access to the internet, television, weather predictions, and more.

THE SPACE RACE

"The Space Race" refers to the period when the United States and the Soviet Union competed to create the best space technology. During the space race, aerospace engineers in both countries worked to build spacecraft that could get a person on the moon. In 1969, the United States "won" the space race when Apollo 11 successfully landed on the moon's surface.

Aerospace engineers work on satellites of all shapes and sizes. Most satellites need a power source, like a battery, as well as an antenna, or a metal rod or wire used to send and receive radio waves that carry information. Aerospace engineers build and maintain these parts of a satellite, making sure satellites collect and send the correct data.

AEROSPACE ENGINEERS IN THE SOVIET UNION, NOW KNOWN AS RUSSIA, BUILT THE FIRST SATELLITE. THIS SATELLITE WAS NAMED SPUTNIK I AND LAUNCHED IN 1957. THE SATELLITE'S LAUNCH KICKED OFF THE SPACE RACE BETWEEN THE SOVIET UNION AND THE UNITED STATES.

23

THE MANY LANGUAGES OF AEROSPACE

There are many ways to "speak" aerospace. It may be useful for engineering hopefuls to learn languages other than English. This can help engineers work for companies in other countries. Some of the biggest aerospace manufacturers are in Russia, Japan, Europe, and the United States. Students interested in aerospace engineering can focus on the languages spoken in those areas.

But there's another type of language engineers may want to learn—programming! Students interested in the technology and computer engineering side of aerospace should look into programming classes. In these classes, you will learn many different ways to code, or write computer programs. Knowing how to code is a good skill for future engineers.

PROGRAMMING LANGUAGES

There are many different programming languages. Some companies use the C/C++ programming languages for their space technology. They might also use Python, another programming language, to code their designs. These programming languages take a long time to master. If you're interested in learning how to code, get started now!

NOT ALL AEROSPACE ENGINEERS NEED TO LEARN HOW TO CODE, BUT THOSE INTERESTED IN THE COMPUTER AND TECHNOLOGY SIDE OF ENGINEERING SHOULD LEARN HOW TO WRITE COMPUTER PROGRAMS.

INTERESTING INNOVATIONS

The world of aerospace has also brought us many inventions. This is all thanks to the **innovation** of aerospace engineers!

Aerospace engineers have created many items that we use in our everyday lives, such as memory foam, which is now often used in mattresses. NASA engineers made memory foam when they were trying to find a way to keep pilots safely cushioned during flight.

An aerospace engineer also created the cochlear implant, a type of hearing aid that uses aerospace technology to help people with hearing loss to hear. The cochlear implant's inventor, engineer Adam Kissiah, also had hearing loss.

CLEAN WATER

Did you know NASA engineers also helped create water filters? Astronauts sometimes spend months in space. NASA needed a way to make sure their astronauts still had access to drinkable water. In the 1970s, NASA engineers and an Oregon research company built a water filter that used iodine, a type of **chemical**, to clean water.

GLOBAL POSITIONING SYSTEMS (GPS) HELP PEOPLE NAVIGATE, OR FIND THEIR WAY. SPACE SATELLITES, BUILT BY AEROSPACE ENGINEERS, POWER THE GPS APPS ON OUR CELL PHONES AND IN OUR CARS.

SHOOT
FOR THE MOON

Over the years, aerospace engineers have dreamed up new ways to go to new places and explore far beyond the clouds. We made it to the moon, thanks to the work of aerospace engineers. But there are still more places to go. As technology improves, humans may be able to travel beyond the moon. Right now, we have only been able to send unmanned **rovers** to planets that far away.

But one day, maybe with your help and hard work, we can put people on those planets, too. As far as science can tell, space is never-ending—which means the work of an aerospace engineer is never truly done!

THE MARS ROVERS

NASA aerospace engineers have been building rovers to collect data from moons and planets, including Mars. Mars is too far away for people to travel to. The planet's environment is also unsafe for human bodies. Since humans can't visit Mars yet, aerospace engineers have built rovers that can safely explore the planet instead.

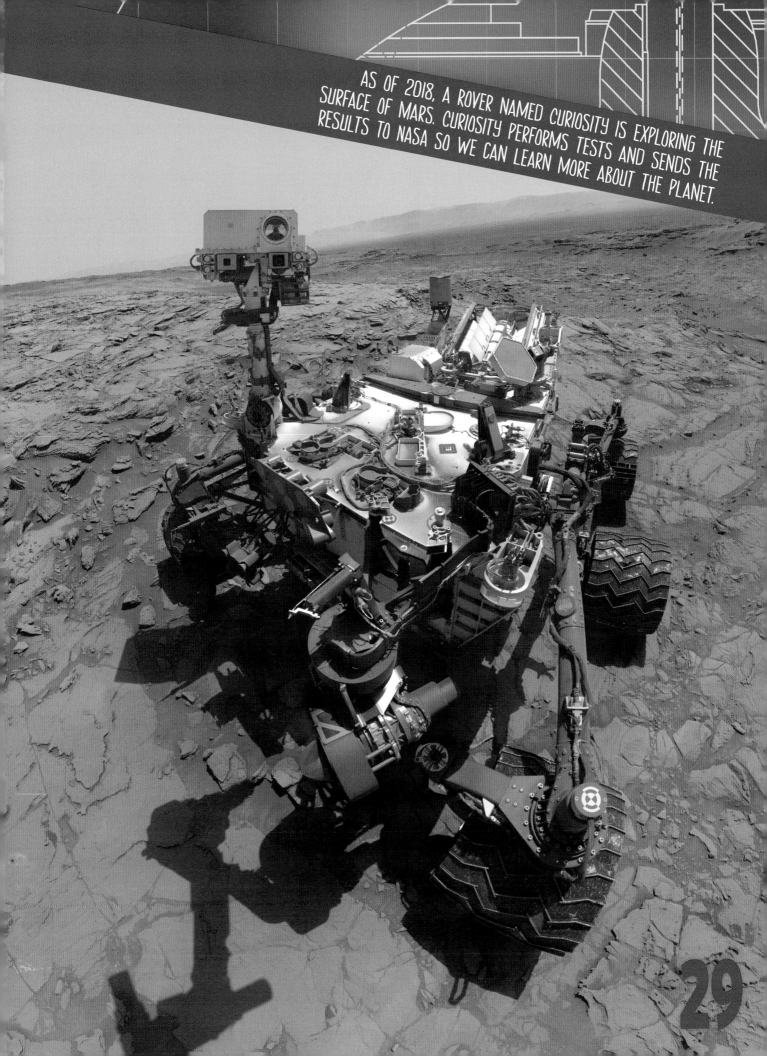

AS OF 2018, A ROVER NAMED CURIOSITY IS EXPLORING THE SURFACE OF MARS. CURIOSITY PERFORMS TESTS AND SENDS THE RESULTS TO NASA SO WE CAN LEARN MORE ABOUT THE PLANET.

GLOSSARY

accident: an unexpected event that happens by chance

astronaut: someone who works or lives in space

characteristic: quality that makes something different from other things

chemical: matter that can be mixed with other matter to cause changes

engineer: someone who plans and builds machines

gravity: the force that pulls objects toward the center of a planet or star

innovation: a new invention or a new way of doing things

mechanical: having to do with machines

physics: the study of matter, energy, force, and motion, and the relationship among them

rover: an object with wheels that explores an environment, like the moon

satellite: an object that circles Earth in order to collect and send information or aid in communication

technology: tools, machines, or ways to do things that use the latest discoveries to fix problems or meet needs

unmanned: not having or needing an onboard crew

FOR MORE INFORMATION

BOOKS

Di Piazza, Domenica. *Space Engineer and Scientist Margaret Hamilton*. Minneapolis, MN: Lerner Publishing, 2017.

Roby, Cynthia. *Building Aircraft and Spacecraft: Aerospace Engineers*. New York, NY: PowerKids Press, 2016.

Waxman, Laura Hamilton. *Aerospace Engineer Aprille Ericsson*. Minneapolis, MN: Lerner Publications, 2015.

WEBSITES

Aerospace Engineers – Science Buddies
www.sciencebuddies.org/science-engineering-careers/engineering/aerospace-engineer
Find out key facts about becoming an aerospace engineer, get project ideas for some hands-on learning, and more.

Intro to Engineering – National Geographic
www.nationalgeographic.org/media/nasa-kids-intro-engineering/
Watch videos about aerospace engineering and explore the field to see if it's a good fit for you!

More to Explore! – NASA Education
www.nasa.gov/audience/forstudents/k-4/more_to_explore/index.html
Find games to play, videos to watch, things to make, and stories to read for students interested in aerospace engineering.

INDEX